BABY, ALL THOSE CURVES
AND ME WITH NO BRAKES

BABY, ALL THOSE *curves*

AND ME WITH NO BRAKES

500 new pickup lines for men and women

STEPHAN DWECK
& MONTERIA IVEY
INTRODUCTION BY
QUEEN LATIFAH

HYPERION
NEW YORK

Library of Congress Cataloging-in-Publication Data

Dweck, Stephan.
Baby, all those curves and me with no brakes : 500 new pickup lines for men and women / Stephan Dweck and Monteria Ivey.
p. cm.
ISBN 0-7868-8274-3
1. Afro-American wit and humor. 2. Man-woman relationships—Humor. 3. Interpersonal communication—Humor. 4. Dating (Social customs)—Humor. 5. Black English. 6. Americanisms. I. Ivey, Monteria. II. Title.
PN6231.N5D93 1998
818'.5402—dc21   97–22736
                                                                                        CIP

Designed by Jill Gogal
First Edition
10 9 8 7 6 5 4 3 2 1

To my boys Chester Mapp, Al Dotson Jr., Roy Smith Jr., Eugene Poston, Eddie Ogarro, and the Douglass Crew. We never grew up, but we never stop growing.

—L. Stephan Dweck

To Shawn, the woman formerly known as aggressive, who keeps me sane in her own crazy way. And to all the family and friends who have supported me in all my artistic endeavors. God bless.

—Monteria Ivey

Contents

To our editor, Leslie Wells

Thanks for keeping us on track and keeping the faith.

We appreciate the support of these people

Queen Latifah, The Flava Unit Family, Nancy Yost, Barbara Lowenstein, Donna Campbell, Yalda Teheranian, Dedra Tate, Jerome Leventhal, Veronica Webb, Karen and Howard Baldwin, Michael Lewittes, Matthew Jordan Smith, Channing Johnson, Kendall Minter, Jason Spitz, Sandy Epstein, The Endeavor Agency, David Colden, Irene Dreyer, Suzanne DePasse, Bob Weinstein, Cary Granat, Gary Sharfin, Michelle Thomas, Warrington Hudlin, Howard Dolgon, E.R. Ship, Imus, Bernard McGirt, Bart Bartolomeo, Donnie Simpson, Jackie Allen, Tracy Jordan, JoJo Pada, Chip, Audra Jones, Marilyn Artis, Shari Headley, Alan Taylor, The Motown Cafe, Helena Echegoyen, Connie Johnson, Reggie Rouse, Christopher Lambert, Maureen Gallagher, LL Cool J

Research Assistants

Shigeru McPherson, Chester Mapp

BABY, ALL THOSE CURVES
AND ME WITH NO BRAKES

Introduction

People have a never-ending fascination with relationships. From movies to television to relationship books to kickin' it with your friends, everybody's talking, because everybody's looking for love.

Of course, everything begins with the art of the pickup line. When it comes down to who has the best lines, Black men are the most poetic. Black men are off the hook, because they do not allow the time and the place to stop them. Latin men are more passionate with their lines. They try to kick the real shit, with a lot of feeling. White guys don't have too many lines. They just try to join in on your conversation. There's no "Hey, baby . . . " unless he's Italian. Italian men have a lot in common with the brothers.

A man with money doesn't have to say much. One look at his wardrobe, especially the shoes, pretty much tells you all you need to know. The guy with no money feels the need to have the better lyric. In either case, a sense of humor is very important. Make me laugh, please. If I'm out socializing I don't want to be serious all the time.

We all want to find our soul mate. Sometimes we get caught up in the confusion between looking for a soul mate and looking for sex. When we first hook up with someone it's all good. There is an infatuation period in the beginning. Eventually this wears down, and you come to realize that this person is completely wrong for you. Then you have to decide to stick it out or move on.

A lot of people get caught up in "garbage" relationships. That's a relationship that you need to throw out, but you find it hard to let go. You're afraid to hurt somebody's feelings, or you have a fear of being alone. So you play it safe, and stay. This just opens the door for people to stray. There's a chance that either person can stray, but guys are more likely to try. Women tend to be more respectful of the relationship, and take the time to think about the consequences. Men are ten times hornier than women. They follow their smaller head more than their bigger head. If a woman is out there she's more "covert," and her guy will never know if she doesn't want him to. Men get impulsive and sloppy, and that's why they get busted.

Here's some advice for the guys: Before you try to get next to us you need to find out who you are first. Women can see through the games, so stop fronting. Too many men feel they have to hide their feelings. They really do want a woman they can express themselves with. Don't get caught up in peer pressure and start believing the hype of false images. Show the real side, and forget about all this dominant, undefeatable, macho crap. Keep it real. Remember, there are different types of women out there. A high maintenance woman isn't for everybody. But women are not all bitches and hoes, or even all goody-goody.

For the ladies, feel free to pick and choose. If you are looking to meet someone, don't go by just a line. Liars will lie to you just as easily as they lie to others. Look through the lines, and pick up on the vibe. Do you like his style? Does he make you laugh? A lot of times we don't know what we're looking for, so you don't have to settle for the first man that pops up. Take a number. Keep in touch. Hang out together for a little while. Within two weeks, you'll find out the basic traits. If he flies off the handle and starts choking the McDonald's lady, you know he'll choke you too. So let him go if you have to.

Trust me on this: If you give a man enough time he'll show you his true colors. I remember once when I was hanging out with another rapper at Nell's in New York, and we met this guy.

He was well hung, and we were taking turns freakin' him on the dance floor. Everything was cool until we went to the ladies' room . . . and he followed us. I asked him, "Do you realize you're in the ladies' room?" He didn't care. That's when I knew I was dealing with a sicko. "Security!"

One last thing. A lot of people get hooked up in the winter because they don't want to be alone. Be careful! In the spring, they'll start feeling extra frisky because they want to be free in the summer. Learn to distinguish between wants versus needs. Your mate needs to know what you need, or else whatever you got going will crumble. If your needs are not being taken care of, then maybe it isn't worth it. If that is the case, you don't have to do something foul, like stop calling and drop off the planet. Face the music, talk it out, and move on to something better.

—Queen Latifah

From the Authors' Corner

We'd like to start by thanking all the people who have supported us in our efforts to tickle the world's funny bone in a unique (and soulful) way. As any author will tell you, once you satisfy your own conditions of satisfaction and send your work out into the public, you just hope that someone else will enjoy reading it as much as you enjoyed writing it. We have been overwhelmed by the response to *You're So Fine, I'd Drink a Tub of Your Bathwater.* We have received letters and e-mail from across the country as well as Canada, Great Britain, New Zealand, South Africa, and the Caribbean. Thanks to international media coverage (with a big assist from our good buddy, supermodel, and fellow author Veronica Webb), men all over the world are now on notice that women have been, are, and always will be one step ahead of us when it comes to understanding the art of the pickup line.

We would be remiss if we did not make note of the fact that our work has not received universal acceptance. Criticism does not faze us. After all, as Harry S. Truman said, "If you can't stand the heat, get out of the kitchen." What does concern us is when those supposedly "in the know" completely miss the boat when trying to categorize our work. We are first, and foremost, humorists. We seek to entertain, and hopefully enlighten, through laughter. Our take on the relationship game comes from this perspective, with a tip of the hat to the sheer artistry and verbal-linguistic dexterity that is the African-American experience. We are not part of the "self-help," "relationship therapy" industry (though judging from their book sales, and infomercial success, maybe we should be).

We are not laying down the "rules," or attempting to establish which planets men and women come from. In our world, people are funny. And the people who try to meet people are the funniest people in the world.

For the benefit of all the guys (because we do have to look out for one another), here's what Ivey and Dweck have learned from interviewing over three hundred women from across the country. Take it with a grain of salt and a dash of common sense.

One, *don't take yourself too seriously.* A sense of humor is essential. Remember, a pickup line is the ice-breaker, not the end-all. If you can get the woman to laugh or smile, then the door is open to pursue further conversation. This isn't brain surgery, so lighten up.

Two, *keep it real.* It's not just a hip-hop expression. In the "getting to know you" game, it is reality. The majority of women surveyed said that they don't care where a man comes from, in terms of money, education, blue collar, white collar, etc. They just don't want a man who is pretending to be something that he is not. In other words, don't say it if you don't mean it.

Three, *if at first you don't succeed . . .* Even Tiger Woods can't make every shot. Okay, you were smooth, charming, and witty. You had a smile in your heart, but you ended up with egg on your face. Get over it. Every dog has his day, but only if he continues to chase the cat. Relationships are not an exact science. If you believe differently, then "get your credit card ready to call the number on the screen."

We hope you enjoy the book. If you're out there looking, maybe we can help. If you have someone, you can share some laughs and reminisce. If you're hangin' with your friends, you can compare notes. And the next time you see that woman you just have to talk to, take a deep breath and say, "Oh baby, all those curves and me with no brakes."

booty LINES

Can I touch your tummy, cuz I love the taste of nuts & honey.

16

Can I have the number to your ass so I can make a booty call?

Would it be possible for you to sit on my face before you told me your name?

If your ass was a table, I'd lay my drink on you.

Baby, your jeans are so loose, do you think I can fill them in with you?

Talk to me, and I promise nothing will happen unless you want it to.

Damn, you got some big legs, girl. Can I get between them?

Damn, baby! That boomin' booty could hurt somebody . . . hopefully me!

When I look into your eyes I feel like I should rip your clothes off.
Comeback: And when I look into your eyes I feel like I should call the police.

I will make love to you so good your toes will curl up.

I'm good to my woman and better to my lover.

You're thick and zesty like Heinz ketchup.

I have nine inches. I can make you very happy.
Comeback: I'm packing twelve inches because I always travel with my ruler.

If I get into you, they'll have to use a crane to get me out.

Girl, I love a big woman because you can keep me warm in the winter.

Do you work as hard in the bedroom as you do in the boardroom?

I'm having you for dinner, and you're having me for dessert.

I'm just saying, baby, would you be the syrup to my pancakes?

Damn, baby, you got enough shake to make an earthquake.

19

Can we get our freak on?

Please, baby, be my freak tonight.

You make my dick hard just by passing me.

Tell me where you want me to put it.
Comeback: Back in the can with the rest of the Vienna sausages.

Are those Boss jeans you got on? Can I see who's really the boss in those jeans?

You look so good I'll eat you right now.

I'll eat the pie if you add the whipped cream.

Damn, baby, can I have it my way, right away?

You look good and I look good, *so why don't we* get together and see if it feels good!

Hey, baby, mo' better, mo' better, mo' better!

Can I be that ice cream that you're licking?

Boy, I would like to be that candy in your mouth.

21

What's up, Boo. Can I get between your legs tonight?

Baby, I want to taste your toe jam.

You have sexy bedroom eyes. Can I talk to you?

Your legs are too close. Can I help you widen them?

Please come home with me. My dick's calling.

Making love to you would take me three days.
Comeback: I can't wait that long for you to get it up.

I'm thirsty. Can you give me some of that milk?

Boy, I would sure like to read the label on your panties.

Baby, I'll move your toes if you make my Jimmy grow.

I'll move your body cream with my sex machine.

Come by for lunch and I promise that I'll be served hot.

I would love to eat you, no strings attached.

Baby, your lips could make my lollipop happy.

Girl, I would love to be the seat in those pants.

Can I lick that caramel complexion of yours?

I wish I was the one sleeping in your bed.

Would you go out with me if I could see through your clothes?
Comeback: No, but there would be a job opening for you in Metropolis.

Damn, baby, I'd like to be that gum you're chewing on.

Can the three of us get together this weekend, you, me, and your tank top?

25

Baby, why don't you slip out of those wet clothes and into a dry martini?

Can I come for lunch and eat you too?

My bed is cold. Do you want to change that?

I wish I was your washcloth so I could be all over your body.

I love big women like you so you can slap me, punch me, kick me, and bite me.

27

You're so hot, you melt the elastic in my underwear.

Would you be my love buffet so I can lay you on the table and take what I want?

28

Is it hot in here, or is it just you?

I miss my teddy bear. Would you sleep with me?

Excuse me, is that semen in your hair?

You know, I've got the f, the c, and the k, so all I need is you.

They say the body's 98 percent water . . . and I'm kinda thirsty.

My fine chocolate thickness, you need a full body rub.

I will love you so hard and deep that I'll fertilize *OUR* seed.

I want you to call me big daddy and scream my name.

Do your lips taste as good as they look?

You look like butter-scotch, and I just love the taste of butter-scotch.

Hey, you . . . yeah, you with the big behind.

Girl, you've got a body like a Coke bottle, and I want you to quench my thirst.

I'll be your bread if you'll be my butter.

Do you think your boyfriend would mind if I spent the night with you so you could lick me all over?

All the others will call you the prettiest in sight, but I'll be honest and tell you that I want you for tonight.

You have the perfect size breasts. What's your name, shorty?

Can I take you downtown?

Let me get up in ya!

I just like to eat you up like a hot biscuit.

32

Shorty, you the bacon, eggs, steak, and collard greens.

I'll make you see the stars.

Come sit on my lap, and I'll let you put a lip lock on my love bone.

Chocolate, honey, sugar, and sweet. Girl, you're so fine you look good enough to eat.

Are you old enough to keep me out of jail?

Girl, I'd like to lick you like a Fudgesicle.

LINES

that get you noticed

Can you sit on my face and let me guess your weight?

Please, please help me. You're so sweet I think I've got diabetes.

With a body and hips like yours, you know you should be carrying my twins.

Is that all yours, or are you on welfare?

I'd marry you tonight, if it wasn't Friday.

Your ass is so big, when you walk, it looks like your ankles are going to break.

Excuse me, you got a man? Yeah, well, why don't you make him your ex so I can be the next.

36

You're so fine I'd give you my wife's food stamps.

I sure would like to wash my face with your body.

Jean-Claude van *DAMN!* You fine!

37

Hey, baby, can you take this pork chop to my house and cook it?

There are two people who love you, and both of them are me.

Is that your ass or does your back have the mumps?

Girl, you're so fine if I can't be your man, then let me be your girlfriend.

Why don't you take off your glasses so I can see your soul?

Hey, miss, I want to marry you—I need a green card.

You are a cool, cool girl in a cool, cool town. You need a cool, cool boy to cool you down.

I've just had a hard day at work. I wish I had someone waiting at home for me.
Comeback: Have you considered a puppy?

Hey, girl. You're cute and sexy, and I have a legal job. What more could we want?

Girl, I'll love you so good, your momma will feel it.

Hey, girl, how about lettin' my Mr. Goodbar get with your Milky Way?
Comeback: Why, so we can have a Baby Ruth that you'll claim isn't yours?

As selective as I am, you have to be special for me to step to you.

Comeback: As selective as I am, I'd have to be desperate to fall for a line like that.

I'm just regrouping from a messy divorce.

Sexy, can I suck your toes?

You fit the description of the girl my mom wants me to marry.

I like slim girls because they are very flexible.

Can I take a picture of your lips?

If I were your underwear, I'd be happy for the rest of my life.

Your knockers are bigger than Jupiter!

Age ain't nothin' but a number, and I like older women.

Girl, can I taste your lips? I don't want to kiss you, I just want to know what fine wine taste like.

Girl, you so fine you make Tina Turner look ugly.

Chocolate is chocolate, curls are curls. If you just give me one chance to spend the night with you, I'll make you feel like a pearl.

Can I count the freckles on your face?

Baby, I'll leave my girl right now for your number.

Is that rump roast the main course or dessert?

43

The fish may die, the river may dry, but my love for you will never die.

I'll take care of you, your kids, and your husband.

If that's what hell looks like, Satan take me with you.

You look like a smothered pork chop.

DAMN!!! Can I bite you? Please?

Yo! Shorty with a forty!

Hey, baby, your eyes are so sexy. Do you have cats in your family?

I would give you my whole check before taxes with no question.

Damn, baby, it looks like you got your whole family on your back.

Baby, leave your man. I'll take care of you and your kids.

You're a beautiful woman trapped in a more beautiful woman's body.

Do I know you from the hospital? Were you my nurse?

You're like sunshine. Please don't rain on my parade.

You have a nice body. Can I be the one to bless it?

Baby, those shorts make your butt look finger-lickin' good.

I spotted you from across the room, and I could tell you wanted me.

I'd love to wrap my arms around your chubby body.

I wish I was one of your tears so I could be born in your eye, run down your cheek, and die on your lips.

Hi, I make more money than you can spend.

I'm new in town . . . could you give me the directions to your apartment?

Do you have a map? I just got lost in your eyes.

Ooh, shorty, you got big feet. I wish you was my girl so we could share our kicks.

Oh, baby, can I go home with you forever?

You got the butt that can stop traffic.

The minute I saw you I knew we were going to get married.

You work and I'll have the children.

Baby, you make me want to shave my head and get a job.

Roses are red, violets are blue, God must have been doin' the do when He made you.

If I was your bread, would you be my water?

You're so pretty. Are you a model? Because I'm an agent.

The Lord is my shepherd. I see what I cannot have.

All that meat and no rice to go with it.

i-know-i'm-ugly,but-i-need-a-date

LINES

I would love for you to have my baby.
Comeback: Thank God for birth control.

Baby, I'll pay your rent, your mother's rent, and feed all of Bebe's kids for a walk in the park with you.

Baby, let me be your "Mr. Clean," and I'll wash your hair, clip your nails, and suck your toes for free.

Your eyes are as pretty as my cat's.
Comeback: And your rap reminds me of kitty litter.

Girl, you remind me of a good cup of coffee: black, strong, and just what I need to start my day.

I would like to be a tooth in your mouth so I can always get licked.

Do you like raisins? How about a date?

What's wrong? You're looking a little sad and gloomy. What you need is some vitamin me.

Can I treat you to dinner and suck you like a neckbone?

54

It's okay if you don't want me. I'll get with your sister just to keep it in the family.

I feel like Richard Gere: I'm standing next to you, the Pretty Woman.

I think you're the most beautiful girl I've seen . . . on a Wednesday.

I don't want a relationship. I just want sex.

If lovin' you is a sin, let the devil come and get me.

I thank heaven for little girls, but who do I thank for the mommas?

Is you mother a baker? Because she created a beautiful piece of cake.

I don't usually stop females in the street, but I was drawn to you.
Comeback: I don't usually laugh in men's faces, but I'll make an exception for you.

Let's make a baby first, then talk.

Honey, you're so fine, you make onions cry.

What does your man have to do with me?
Comeback: Why don't you ask him? He's right behind you.

If you guess my age, I'll buy you a drink. If you don't, I'll still buy you a drink.

I'd like to check your tonsils with my tongue.

I cannot finish my meal unless you tell me your name. *Comeback:* Waiter. Check, please.

Hiya! Care for a sucker to love you forever?

57

My tongue is on the most wanted list.

If you got a man, don't worry: We'll keep it on the down-low.

Girl, you definitely is a dime. I'm gonna walk with you and give you all my time.

Baby, you are so fine I'd like to do your laundry.

If you'll just talk to me for a moment, I'm sure it will change my life.

Haven't you seen me on TV?
Comeback: Yes, "America's Most Wanted."

If beauty were gold, I'd claim you on my taxes.

I don't care if you have a boyfriend because I'm not the jealous type.

You've got the prettiest lips ever. Be my woman—and I'll never stop kissing you!

Do you have a mom? If so, can I date both of you?

Do you have a man? When you're finished with him, come to me.

Yo, shorty, you look good, but if you be with me, I can make you look better than that!

Hey, chocolate, can I be your chip?

You're so fine I'll kiss the ground you walk on.

59

I will cook, I'll clean, I'll iron as long as you'll be with me.

I just came to this country, and I'm looking for someone nice.

Baby, I love you and I want to marry you.

I wanna be with you until death.

Can I get you a candle-light bubble bath with wine on the side?

If you are taken, I would like to know if you have a twin sister.

Hey, baby, you know you want this. I seen you checking me out.

I'd buy a drink, but I don't want to walk to the cash machine.

Don't you know that we could make beautiful babies?

I'm moving out of the country, so can I have your number in case I come back?

If I could guess the first three digits of your phone number, would you give me the rest?

If I could get a job where you work, I'd give up all my benefits.

If you were to be my woman, I'd give you my paycheck every week.

You know, there's been a rumor going around that you're a lesbian.
Comeback: If I had to date you, I would be gay.

Are you religious? Good, 'cause I'm here to answer your prayers.

Hey, you, CoCo Reese's Pieces!

Girl, you look like someone who can cook. Can I come over for dinner?

You smell so good, I wanna follow you home.

Yo, shorty, backyard is banging. Can I please get the digits?

Your lips look finger-lickin' good.

You remind me of my mother. Can we talk?

I'll give you the world just for five minutes of your time.

Your beauty stops my heart. How about some CPR?

Excuse me, can I have your autograph?

You are funny, and you are sexy . . . you got to be mine!

If you look this good, I wanna meet your pops.

Damn, baby, you're so thick.

God bless your mother for those good looks.

I just know you are the type of girl who can rock my world.

I need a wife like a car needs wheels. Will you be mine?

Your mom shouldn't trust you here alone.

Miss, I'll give you anything you want. I'm better than your man.

I'd rather take you than a million dollars.

I could take you to a higher level than your man.

If you look like your daddy, then he got to look good!

Um, excuse me. Is it fine in here, or is it just you?

Hey, baby! What do I have to do to make that all mine?

The way you walk, baby, you just make me want to love you all night.

Can I have your number? I just want to invite you to one of my VIP parties.

I'd cry ten buckets of water for you.

I've got tickets to a show and nobody to go with.

Honey, you must be a genie, because all my wishes just came true.

If this is true love, I'm hooked.

Can I borrow your pen and give me your number?

Yo, you look good. Come here. Let me politic wit' you for a minute.

70

Is this building for models? Because if it is, I want to move in.

drive-by
LINES

Hey, girl, dump that Swiss and get with this cheddar.

I'm no dog, but I'll let you walk me to your house.

If you were a bone, I would be your dog.

Baby, if you was my rice and beans, I'd eat every grease spot.

Girl, you so fine you make me wanna run through the woods butt-naked just to get a smile.

If looks could kill, your ass would've been dead a long time ago.

I'd love to be your panties.

Comeback: Why? You're already full of shit.

Forget about that dog. Why don't you put me on that leash?

Girl, you know you're the finest woman on this block. Can you hook a brother up?

Comeback: Sorry, I don't have any spare change.

Hey, honey, is that real back there, or is it a pillow where I can rest my head?

With a body like that you could kill a man.

Girl, you got the prettiest smile. Call me collect.

Baby, you so fine, my dog's in heat.

Why don't you "hello" me if you want to get to know me!
Comeback: Goodbye.

Damn, baby! I'm chillin' like a villain. What's your number?

Where you going, my African queen?
Comeback: Back to Africa.

Slow down and talk to me before I give you a ticket for speeding.

77

If you want to get with a winner, you need to drop that man I call a chicken dinner.

Hello. My name is Big Daddy. Beep me tonight.

Excuse me, didn't we go to school together?
Comeback: No, I never attended reform school.

Girl, I want to hit it, split it, and never quit it.

Girl, you remind me of my car: I wanna wax it, pump it, and ride it, baby.

You look so good I'll park my Lexus just to walk with you.

If you have a man, I hope you have a twin.

Oh, yes! You're definitely a dime. Can you spare a minute of your time?

Excuse me. Are you too tall for a short conversation?

Hey, baby, I'll take you and your debts.

Baby, you have an ass that a man would be happy to come home to.

Baby, I could not help but notice the design on your jeans, so I thought I'd come over and get a better look.

Is your last name Campbell, because you look "um, um, good."

You're so fine I had to make a U-turn on a one-way street.

If you cook as well as you walk, I'll even eat the crumbs.

Baby, this walk of yours drives me crazy.

Hi! How are you doing? Fine? I know you're fine, but how are you doing?

Hey! Yo! What's up? Me and you, baby!

Can I talk to you for a second?

Baby, don't walk by me: I'll die without knowing your name.

Can I walk you home?

You so fly you could take all my money.

If you were a car, I would ride you.
Comeback: And if you were a plate, I'd drop you.

Yo! You mad pretty, yo!

God bless your beautiful big body.

You're the right one to take home to momma.

Your name must be Candy because you look so sweet.

Just give me a minute and I'll give you the world.

Can you direct me? I'm trying to get to Lovers' Lane.

One look at you made me forget my name.

Damn, shorty, you look wild, but I could tame you.

If you need a ride, I could put you on my back.

God bless your ass.

Hey, brown sugar. Come, let me kiss your feet.

Hey, baby. Let me take you to meet my mommy.

Excuse me. Do you know which way is New Jersey?

Your daughter is cute, but her mother is even cuter.

Would you like to ride in my new car?

Are those Bugle Boy jeans you're wearing?

You live in the neighborhood?

That walk is dangerous. Please don't hurt me.

You're too pretty to be walking with your head down.

Any man who would let you walk alone doesn't deserve you.

You're too attractive to look so mean.

I have never had my breath taken away like this.
Comeback: Sounds like asthma to me.

Never before did I believe in love at first sight.

Hello, honey. With that body you can spend all my money.

85

When I laid eyes on you it was like a spiritual awakening.

Shorty, are you lost? 'Cause you can just take my hand and follow me.

You're so fine, I'll marry you right now!

Hello, Miss Sweet Thang.

Hey, sunshine! How are you doing today?

Girl, you look sweeter than a Georgia peach.

86

Let's swing a love thing every day, all day.

I know this is going to sound like a line, but did that sound like a line? Are you disappointed? *Comeback:* Yes.

Your name should be Jiggie because you are the bomb-diggie.

Milk does the body good, but I could do you better.

Hey, chocolate, if you taste as good as you look, I'll lick you all over.

phone
LINES

You know what they say about girls with glasses: They have big asses.

Baby, I'm not looking for love, just a meaningful sexual relationship.

I would love for you to wrap your legs around my neck and squeeze like a python.

You're light, bright, and just my height.

If I had a lady that looked as good as you, coming home would not be the problem.

One night with you and I would never look at another woman.

90

Girl, you're so sweet, strawberries need sugar just to keep up.

I hope you know I'm try-ing to come on to you.

Comeback: I hope you know I'm not interested.

Can I have a taste of your juice so I can bring out the magic in my soul?

Your lips are so juicy. May I kiss you?

I had a dream last night, and you were in it.

What numbers can I dial so I can see your pretty face again?

Oh, baby! Name, number, and please say yes.

How could your old man ever let you go?

I'll give you a dollar to talk for five minutes.

Can I call you to make sure you got home safe?

Damn, you're so sweet. Too bad I'm diabetic.

You so fine my heart just skipped a beat.

Girl, you can drive me to drink, you're so fine.

Hi. Before I meet you, could I meet your lips?

Can I have a bite of your strawberry?

Can I come to your house and jump your bones?

As long as the both of us have nothing to do, why not do it together?

You're the type of girl my doctor recommended.

Sweetheart, I eat, sleep, and drink you. Why won't you let me help you?

Honey, you've got the look I want to know better.

Girl, you is like a sweet cherry pie. Can I have a slice?

You are the finest thing I've ever seen. I'd marry your daddy.

Girl, you are so fine I'm blinded by your beauty.

I would say God bless you, but he already did.

Girl, you look and smell like fine wine.

train LINES

"Miss, do you have the time?" "Yes. It's 2:30." "No, I mean time for me."

You got a man. I got a girl. So let's get together and let them find each other.

Shorty, you look so good. If you were an ice-cream cone, I wouldn't let you melt.

Last night I had a dream about you, but I woke up right before you gave me your number.

My father is mixed with Puerto Rican, so I promise we'll have a baby with good hair.

Your eyes are so beautiful, I get lost in them.

My friend wanted to know if you are available.

Can I be your shadow?

You look so sweet I get a cavity just looking at you.

I'm so in love with you, I'd kill three people to go out with you.

I would love to take you home to my mother.

You have beautiful legs. Do you run track?

Jesus Christ, what a woman.

I love the gap between your teeth.

100

Can I have a light and your phone number?

Your butt is so round it looks like a basketball.

You're so fine you make my heart dance.

You're so attractive—I look at you and my juices flow.

Girl, I bet your man has fun with them big legs.

Hey, Brown Sugar Baby, I get high off your love.

Can I be the ice cream on your cone?

101

Hey, chocolate. You want some sprinkles?

I know you can't be that bow-legged. I must be cock-eyed.

What are my chances to get my hair done like yours?

You're so beautiful that I have to put on sunglasses to look at you.

I will pay you for looking at your sexy body.

I wouldn't mind being those tight pants of yours.

103

you're not going to believe these **LINES**

Baby, your ass sits up like two peaches.

If I was starving and you were a Big Mac, I would die of hunger just to let you flaunt your beauty.

Your legs are so pretty that Ike Turner wants to beat you.

Hey, chocolate, if you were a Dutch Master, I'd smoke you.

You gots some nice tits. *Comeback:* And you've got some big balls to try a line like that.

Are you breastfeeding? Can I have some?

107

Can I pull on your hair to see if it's real?

Comeback: Can I pull on your dick to see if it's really that small?

Your lips are so big I think of J.J. when I look at them.

Damn, girl, your ass is as fine as mine.

Something about you makes me wanna leave my wife, but she pays the bills.

Girl, I want to kiss you and make your teeth come out.

You need a man that can make your toenails do inverted flips.

Hey, girl, come sit on my face and let me eat my way to your heart.

You have nice legs. Can I shave them?

You look so good I'll smell your farts.

Me and my dog want you for tonight.

Girl, you look so fine, I could stick my dick in your ear.
Comeback: That's okay. I already have a Q-Tip.

Didn't I see you on "America's Most Wanted"? Because I want you.

Baby, you are so beautiful, you make Vanessa Williams look like Aunt Esther from "Sanford and Son."

Girl, I can have you whipped up in a white dress, in a house, and barefoot with a muffin in the oven in two minutes.

Your lips are so sexy and hot that they melt the butter on my mashed potatoes.

I'll pay your rent, buy your clothes, get your hair and nails done. . . . All I need is a job.

If I was twenty years younger, I'd give you the world for about twenty minutes.

You look just like this guy I used to know. What's your name anyway?

Hey, girl, your moustache is turning me on.

Oh, girl, I would love to take you out, but I'm so broke I can't even buy you a chicken wing.

111

You have a baby scent smell.

Comeback: You mean I smell like shit?

Baby, you look so good, you're the reason why I'm against abortion.

You so fly, you need to jump back and kiss yourself.

Damn, girl! You're short and stocky and built like Rocky.

I know you didn't think you were gonna walk over here with all that luggage and me not say something.

Girl, I've been watchin' you watchin' me watchin' you, and if I get you alone . . . watch out!

Your beauty is so devas- tating that I've fallen and I can't get up.

113

One look at you and I already love my future mother-in-law, and I don't even know her.

The way I make love is like a drug: One dose of this and you're hooked.

Girl, you sure make a black man wanna holler!

You smoke weed, shorty?

I want to eat you until you bleed.

Can I breastfeed them?

Girl, I love the way you move, ya make me want to stick you.

Your shit is like gold and sweeter than honey.

Hi, I work for *Essence* magazine. I'm doing a survey on America's most beautiful women. Can I get your name and number?
Comeback: My name is Satan and my number is 666.

Baby girl, I swear you remind me of my bank account.
Comeback: Yeah, a bounced check and no savings.

Honey, are those your breasts? Because they are bigger than the corns on my feet.

Do you look that good when you wake up in the morning?

A woman your age needs sex, so I will be there for you.

Girl, you so high yellow, you bring sunshine into my life.

Would you please tell me where you live so I could move in?

Can I suck your forehead?

Damn, baby, you're healthy. The bigger the ocean, the better the motion.

Baby, you are so fine, if you were mine, I would put you on my dresser and dust you every day.

When I first saw you it was like déjà vu. I know we were together in another lifetime.

Are you hairy all over?
Comeback: You'll never know.

May I touch your sideburns?

Oh, baby, you are all that and a Big Mac.

I'm in the music industry, and I would love to sample your demo.

I'm no designer, but I would love to see you stroll on my runway.

118

Is that all yours, or did you pay a lot for it?

Who needs drugs when just looking at you makes me high?

119

dead
LINES

You look just like the cousin I always wanted.
Comeback: You look like the pet I always hated.

Hi, I'm born again. Would you like to baptize me?
Comeback: No, but you do need a bath.

Excuse me, did we meet in another life?
Comeback: Yes, I was the hangman at your execution.

Baby, you have the most pretty eyes that I have seen in a long time.
Comeback: And you have the worst syntax I've heard in a long time.

I wish you were my girl so I could have beautiful children like you.

Baby, you need to go out with me. I own a bodega.

Hey, love, buy me a drink and I'll be your man for the night.

123

I want to marry you
because you have long
hair.

Could I give you all my
money and not touch you?

You are so beautiful.
Would you like to help
me carry this carton of
milk?

124

Baby, you look so sweet, sugar just lost its taste.

I don't care what your first name is because your last name is Heaven.

I will marry you tomorrow for a kiss today.

You look so crispy and good that you remind me of a cookie.

Comeback: And you remind me of a wet noodle . . . limp.

Were you born just to torment me with your gorgeous looks?

Oh my God. I done seen the light and she's shining my way.

Hi, will you marry me and live the rest of your life just loving me?

Comeback: No. I don't date vampires.

Promise you won't hurt me, because I've got a weak heart.

126

Hey, Green Eyes, are you as colorful as your eyes?

I've always wanted a short-haired woman.

I feel a special connection between us.

127

You smile like my mother.

Hi. Nice day, even though it's raining.

Girl, I would love to get to know you, but you're too young.

You must be famous because you look like a star to me.

I know you're married, because the pretty ones are all taken.

Baby, you look like a Ring Ding cake: good enough to snack on.

You're pretty; I like you. I would propose to you, but I can't bend my knees!

You are too sexy to be a mother of two.

You look so hot, you make my blood boil.

So, do I look like a cartoon character?
Comeback: Yes. Goofy.

I'd change my religion just to be with you!

I'm married, but we're separated at the moment.

No one has ever fit my arms the way that you do.

Damn, you're fine. Will you marry me?

Move three inches to the left, you sexy thing you.

You look just like my first girlfriend.

130

I got nothing but love for you, baby.

Your are sexy and beautiful, and I want you to be my girl forever.

You're the prettiest person I've ever seen in blue.

Love those sad eyes.

You have some lovely eyes. Can I talk to you, please?

Do you have a twin sister? Because I think I saw you before.

I have a feeling today is your lucky day.

Girl, can I be the sun that shines on your day?

Baby, your eyes remind me of Biggie; they hypno-tize me.

132

Your eyes are so clear I can see into our future.

Even Stevie Wonder can see that you and I belong together.

The chemistry between us could only be labeled "highly flammable."

You shine like a star.

I won't stop asking you out until I hear your mother scream.

You're so fine, not even Picasso could capture your beauty.

133

LINES

and flowers

You're as beautiful as a rose.
Comeback: And you're as irritating as a thorn in my side.

How can I get to meet you to spend my money on you?

Choose me, and I'll give you everything that everybody else can't afford!

Can I fuck your brains out and make you lose control?
Comeback: No, but you could buy a token and ride your ass outta here.

Hi, I'm looking for an intelligent and stable person, and you seem like the one who fits that description.

Girl, you're like the wave I dreamed about in the ocean last night.

If beauty is in the eye of the beholder, I wanna hold you all day long.

I am a faithful guy.
Comeback: Yeah, faithful to your mother.

You're the woman in all my dreams. I've been dreaming about you since I became a man.
Comeback: I guess you haven't been dreaming too long.

I need you like a needle needs a thread.

137

I would pay your bills, massage your feet, and be your love slave.

138

Helen of Troy can send off a thousand ships, but your beauty can bring them all back.

Can I see that label? I just wanted to know if you were made in Heaven.

If you were a plant, I would water you every day.

If you were a tear in my eye, I would not cry for fear of losing you.

Ma'am, I hear you're wanted for stealing my heart.

Hello, sweetness. Before we go any further, I don't want anything from you. I just want to give you the world.

You've just been nominated for the most beautiful woman in the world, next to my mom.

God bless your parents for planting the seed that produced such a lovely flower.

I don't have much, but I'm willing to share.

I could be wrong, but you look like a great person, and I would love to get to know you better.

You are the twinkle in my eyes.

Excuse me. I couldn't help noticing you. My name is Mike. What's yours?

Your beauty can bring out the sun.

140

Damn, baby, you are the beat in my heart.

I'm not a talker, but for you I'll speak to the world.

Hello. I just want to say hello to you. You just made my day.

141

I just want to take you out and wine and dine you.

Sweet African princess, can I know your name?

Hello, young lady, would you like some company?

Baby, if I had one wish, that wish would be me always loving you. I will treat you like the queen that you are.

I would like to get more acquainted with you if you would allow me the pleasure of your presence.

Your eyes are like the brightest star.

If you give me the time, I'll make everything worthwhile.

I'll give you the world on a gold platter.

I like you for your mind and knowledge.

Hello, lady, I love your stylish ways.

You the prettiest girl I ever met.

I've been blessed. Damn, you look good.

Damn, baby, God must have heard me calling you.

You are the flower that grows in my heart.

Baby, I will wine you and dine you, be your chef, your maid, your lover. Just give me a chance.

143

Sweetheart, I'd work three jobs just to take care of all your needs.

A black queen. Can I be your king?

I am a guy who doesn't cheat.

Comeback: I'm a girl who doesn't give any up.

144

I would love you like no other man could.

Hi, sweetheart. You look financially distressed. Do you mind if I take care of you?

I have been waiting for you all my life.

Sweetie, can I hold your hand while we walk and talk?

Just show me the way to your heart, body, and soul, and I'll follow with no exceptions.

146

You have the face I want to wake up to every morning.

I've just melted looking into your eyes.

Hello, could you be the lady of my dreams? *Comeback:* No, but you are the man of my nightmares.

I'll take care of you and your kids.

You look like a rose. I wish you were planted in my garden.

Your smile can be my night-light when I sleep at night.

147

Honey, didn't we meet before at the pear y gates of Heaven?

How you feeling, sweetheart? Can I please have a minute of your time?

Hey, there! You look like the kind of woman I need to complete my life.

If I was a prince, I'd fill you with treasures and make you feel like the true princess you are.

Excuse me, sweetheart, but do you think I can have a minute of your precious time?

"What was that?" "That sound? That was the sound of my heart breaking."

My beautiful queen, you have a strong spiritual aura that's calling for a mate.

You're so fine, I want to help you and be a friend for life.

I don't want anything from you, just friendship.

You're so fine, I want to spend the rest of my life with you and support you.

Your eyes can make a man tell all his innermost secrets.

I can see my future in your beautiful eyes.

Give me your love and I'll give you everything your little heart desires.

Are you an angel? Because you have a heavenly scent.

I'm sorry for bothering you, but I couldn't let a beautiful young lady like yourself walk out of my life.

Beautiful, if you don't have a man at this present time, can I please have the honor and talk to you for a minute.

I'd give you the world if you were mine.

I have a Land Cruiser and a house in the islands.

You seem like an ideal queen. How would you like to get to know an aspiring prince?

Hey, baby, are you sure you didn't fall from the sky? Because I'm sure I just saw a falling star.

I've been waiting all my life to meet you.

naughtiest places people have made love

On top of the copy machine

On my boss's desk

In the supply closet

On the terrace

On the fire escape

On the kitchen counter

In the coat closet

In my parents' bedroom

In the elevator

154

In the basement

On the roof of my building

In Central Park

In the radio broadcast studio

On the stairs in the projects

By the monkey bars in the playground

Backseat of my car

Theater dressing room

In a treehouse

155

On the beach

In a nightclub (during a party)

On top of a big-screen television

In a department store

In a supermarket

On a rowboat

In the swimming pool

Under a bridge

In the doctor's office

On an X-ray machine

In the movie theater

In a restaurant coat-check room

In the library

In a police precinct

In an airplane bathroom

Backseat of a limousine

In a garage

In a police van

157

In a bookstore

School gymnasium

In the laundry room

On the George Washington Bridge

In a jail cell

In a dressing room at Madison Square Garden

Backstage at Carnegie Hall

Orchestra pit at the Met

VD clinic

Funeral/wake

Job interview

Orchestra pit at Carnegie Hall

In a horse-drawn carriage

In a cornfield

On a mountain ledge

In a carwash

At the Grand Canyon

Maintenance room at the "CBS Evening News" studio

We would like your comments on this book as well as any new pickup lines.

I'll Have Two Cheeseburgers and Some Fries, Inc.
P.O. Box 770
New York, New York 10025

or

E-mail us at:
Deacon-Blues@msn.com